CLASSIFYING ANI

Insects

Sarah Wilkes

CLASSIFYING ANIMALS

Titles in this series:

Amphibians Birds Fish Insects Mammals Reptiles

Conceived and produced for Hodder Wayland by

Nutshell
MEDIA

Intergen House, 65–67 Western Road, Hove BN3 2JQ, UK
www.nutshellmedialtd.co.uk

Consultant: Judith Marshall, Natural History Museum
Editor: Polly Goodman
Designer: Tim Mayer
Illustrator: Jackie Harland
Picture research: Morgan Interactive Ltd and Victoria Coombs

Published in Great Britain in 2006 by Hodder Wayland, an imprint of Hodder Children's Books.

This paperback edition published in 2007 by Wayland, an imprint of Hachette Children's Books.

British Library Cataloguing in Publication Data
Wilkes, Sarah, 1964–
Insects. – (Classifying animals)
1. Insects – Classification – Juvenile literature
I. Title
595.7'012

ISBN 978 0 7502 5301 7

Cover photograph: the face of a tree wasp
Title page (clockwise from top left): stag beetle, dragonfly; ladybird; wasp.
Chapter openers: close-up photographs of the scales on four butterfly wings and a compound eye.

Picture acknowledgements
Corbis *Cover* (Robert Pickett), **Ecoscene** 6 (Robin Williams), 7 (Julian Partridge), 14 (Wayne Lawler), 18 (Kjell Sandved), 25 (Chinch Gryniewicz), 40 (Wayne Lawler), 42 (Erik Schaffer), 43 (Tom Ennis); Ecoscene/Papilio 8 (Peter Bond), 10 (Robert Pickett), 11 (William Dunn), 15 (Alastair Shay), 16, 17, 24 bottom (Robert Pickett), 26 (Lando Pescatori/Papilio), 27 (Robert Pickett), 28 (Lando Pescatori), 29 top, 31 (Robert Pickett), 32 (Michael Maconachie), 33 (Mike Buxton), 34 (Robert Pickett), 35 (Robert Gill), 36 top (Peter Bond), 36 bottom (Ken Wilson), 37, 38 (Robert Pickett), 41 (Michael Maconachie); **naturepl.com** 4 (Ingo Arndt), 9 (Richard Bowsher), 12 (Dietmar Nill), 13 (Solvin Zankl), 20 (Duncan McEwan), 21 (John B Free), 22 (John Cancalosi), 23 (Peter Oxford), 24 top (John Downer), 29 bottom (Peter Blackwell), 30 (Mark Payne-Gill).

Printed and bound in China.

Hachette Children's Books
338 Euston Road, London NW1 3BH

CONTENTS

What are Insects? 4

Wingless Insects (Apterygota) 6

Dragonflies and Damselflies (Odonata) 8

Grasshoppers and Crickets (Orthoptera) 10

Mantids and Cockroaches (Dictyoptera) 14

Termites (Isoptera) 18

Earwigs (Dermaptera) 20

Bugs (Hemiptera and Homoptera) 22

Beetles (Coleoptera) 26

Flies (Diptera) 30

Butterflies and Moths (Lepidoptera) 34

Ants, Bees and Wasps (Hymenoptera) 38

Under Threat 42

Insect Classification 44

Glossary 45

Further Information 47

Index 48

Due to the number of insect orders, it is not possible to describe them all in this book. Therefore only the main orders are featured, selected on the basis of the number of species in the order and their significance. All the orders are listed on page 44.

WHAT ARE INSECTS?

INSECTS ARE THE MOST NUMEROUS AND DIVERSE OF ALL animal groups. They are found everywhere in the world, from the tropics to the poles. Scientists have identified at least 2 million species but it is likely that the final total will be in excess of 10 million.

Shared features

Insects belong to the phylum Arthropoda – animals with jointed legs. All arthropods have a tough outer layer covering their body, called an exoskeleton. Their legs are divided into many sections so that they can bend easily. All insects have three body parts: a head, a thorax and an abdomen. Attached to the thorax are three pairs of legs and usually two pairs of wings. The head bears a pair of compound eyes, a pair of antennae, and mouthparts, which are specially adapted to each insect's diet.

Metamorphosis

Insects lay eggs that hatch into larvae. The larvae undergo a number of moults before they become adults. The change from larva to adult is called metamorphosis. Some insects have four stages of change, called complete metamorphosis: egg, larva, pupa and adult. The larva looks very different from the adult. During the pupal stage, the body of the larva changes into that of the adult. Other insects have only three stages of change: egg, nymph and adult, called incomplete metamorphosis. The nymph gradually becomes more like the adult after each moult.

The three body parts of an insect, the head, thorax and abdomen can be seen clearly on this young locust.

CLASSIFICATION

About 2 million different organisms have been identified and sorted into groups, in a process called classification. Biologists look at the similarities and differences between organisms, and those with shared characteristics are grouped together. The largest group is called the kingdom, for example the animal kingdom. Each kingdom is divided into smaller groups, called phyla (singular: phylum). Each phylum is divided into classes, which are divided into orders, then families, genera (singular: genus), and finally species. A species is a single type of organism with unique features that are different from all other organisms, for example a monarch butterfly. Only members of the same species can reproduce with each other and produce fertile offspring.

The classification of a monarch butterfly (*Danaus plexippus*) is shown on the right.

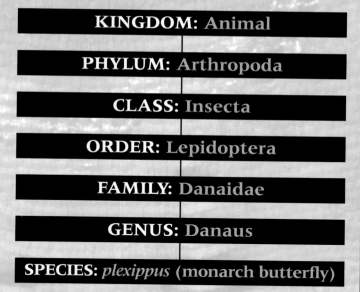

KINGDOM: Animal

PHYLUM: Arthropoda

CLASS: Insecta

ORDER: Lepidoptera

FAMILY: Danaidae

GENUS: Danaus

SPECIES: *plexippus* (monarch butterfly)

One way of remembering the order of the different groups is to learn this phrase:
'**K**ings **P**lay **C**hess **O**n **F**ridays **G**enerally **S**peaking'.

COMPLETE METAMORPHOSIS

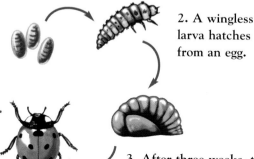

1. A female ladybird lays her eggs on the underside of leaves.

2. A wingless larva hatches from an egg.

4. An adult ladybird emerges from the pupa.

3. After three weeks, the larva turns into a pupa.

INCOMPLETE METAMORPHOSIS

1. A female damselfly lays her tiny eggs in pondweed.

3. The larva spends two years in the water before climbing out. Its skin splits and a winged adult emerges.

2. The egg hatches into an aquatic larva (nymph) which goes through a series of moults.

Insect groups

The class Insecta is divided into two subclasses: wingless insects (Apterygota) and winged insects (Pterygota). Apterygota contains primitive wingless insects that do not go through metamorphosis. The subclass Pterygota consists of winged insects that go through metamorphosis. Within Pterygota there are 27 orders, divided into two groups: Exopterygota, which undergo incomplete metamorphosis, and Endopterygota, which undergo complete metamorphosis.

This books looks at some of the orders of insects, their characteristics and the way each group of insects is adapted to its environment. All the orders are listed on page 44.

WINGLESS INSECTS (APTERYGOTA)

THE SUBCLASS APTERYGOTA CONTAINS ABOUT 600 species of primitive insects that are very different from other insects. The subclass is divided into two orders: bristletails (Archeognatha) and silverfish (Thysanura). The word Archeognatha means 'ancient jaw' and Thysanura means 'fringe tail'.

Apterygota features

Unlike all other insects, bristletails and silverfish do not undergo metamorphosis. The young insects, known as nymphs, look like small adults. They develop by shedding their exoskeleton and growing larger.

Bristletails and silverfish do not have any wings. They are small insects, just 1–1.5 cm (0.4–0.5 in) long. Their bodies are long, flat and tapering. They have three long projections, called cerci (singular: cercus), which extend from the end of the abdomen, making the body look much longer. In bristletails, the middle cercus is the longest, but in silverfish they are the same length. The antennae are particularly long, especially in bristletails. In addition to the three pairs of legs, bristletails have several pairs of short knobs on the abdomen, which may be the remains of additional legs lost through evolution.

The silverfish (*Lepisma saccharina*) gets its name from its covering of shiny scales. Young silverfish resemble adults except they are smaller and white. They become silver at about 6 weeks.

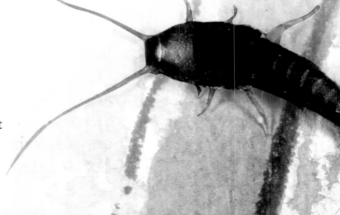

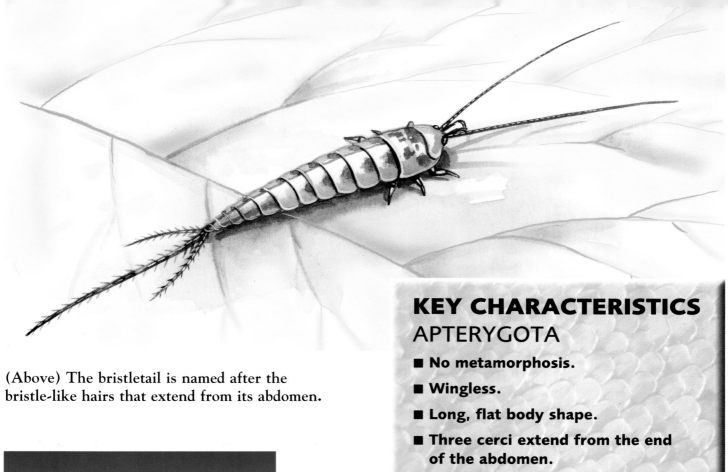

(Above) The bristletail is named after the bristle-like hairs that extend from its abdomen.

KEY CHARACTERISTICS
APTERYGOTA

- **No metamorphosis.**
- **Wingless.**
- **Long, flat body shape.**
- **Three cerci extend from the end of the abdomen.**

The strandline often contains rotting seaweed, shells, dead fish and rubbish, which attracts bristletails and other scavengers such as crabs.

Habitats

Bristletails tend to be found in grassy or woody habitats because they live in leaf litter, the layer of fallen leaves and twigs that carpet the woodland floor, or under bark and stones. They are nocturnal insects that are active at night. Bristletails are herbivores, feeding on plant matter such as algae, moss and lichens, but they will also scavenge on dead and decaying animal material in the leaf litter. Some types of bristletail are found on beaches. There is often a pile of debris on the beach at the high-tide mark, which has been carried in by the tides. This is known as the strandline and bristletails scavenge for food there.

Silverfish are frequently found in houses, especially in kitchens, bathrooms and basements, where it may be damp. Often they are found hiding under carpets. Like bristletails they are nocturnal, emerging at night to feed on crumbs of food dropped on the floor.

DRAGONFLIES AND DAMSELFLIES (ODONATA)

DRAGONFLIES AND DAMSELFLIES ARE BRIGHTLY COLOURED insects found near water. They are among the fastest insect fliers. They are also among the oldest. Fossil remains suggest that they existed 300 million years ago. Dragonflies and damselflies are grouped in the order Odonata, which means 'toothed jaws'. There are more than 5,500 species, which are divided into two suborders: dragonflies (Anisoptera) and damselflies (Zygoptera).

The large eyes of this southern hawker dragonfly (*Aeshna cyanea*) occupy much of the head. Its wings are held out to the side of the body.

Odonata features

Dragonflies are larger than damselflies, with a thicker body. They have two pairs of large, transparent wings that cannot be folded away. The wings are held out when the insect is at rest. The hind pair of wings is slightly wider than the front pair. Each pair of wings can move independently of the other when flying, which means the insect can hover and steer in order to catch prey. Damselflies have two pairs of wings of similar size. Their wings are folded up above their body when at rest.

Damselflies such as this banded demoiselle (*Calopteryx splendens*) have a long, slender body with wings that fold above the body.

Compound eyes

All insects have a pair of compound eyes. Each compound eye is made up of hundreds of tiny, hexagonal units, called ommatidia, each with a corneal lens. Each hexagonal unit functions as a separate eye connected to the insect's brain. Insect eyes see a very different image from that seen by human eyes. They cannot see such a detailed image, but they do detect colours, patterns, shapes and movement. The compound eyes of dragonflies are particularly large and consist of approximately 30,000 units. This provides them with excellent sight. They can judge distances and are sensitive to the slightest movements, which helps them to fly at high speeds through an array of obstacles in pursuit of prey.

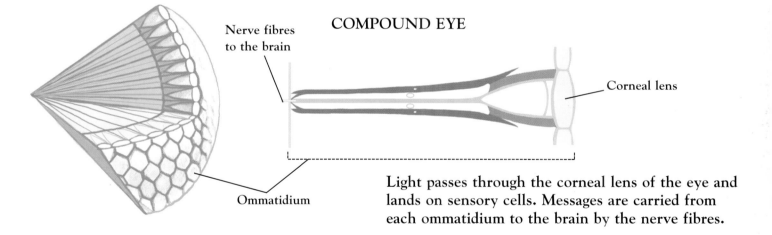

COMPOUND EYE

Nerve fibres to the brain

Corneal lens

Ommatidium

Light passes through the corneal lens of the eye and lands on sensory cells. Messages are carried from each ommatidium to the brain by the nerve fibres.

WHAT'S THE DIFFERENCE?

DRAGONFLY

- **Enormous eyes cover the top and sides of the head.**
- **Wings held straight out beside the body when at rest.**
- **Strong flier.**
- **The nymph is heavy and moves slowly across the mud at the bottom of ponds, lakes and slow-moving streams.**

DAMSELFLY

- **Eyes do not cover the top and sides of the head.**
- **Wings held folded back above the body when at rest.**
- **Weak flier.**
- **The nymph is slender and lives near the surface, among the pondweed.**

Dragonfly nymphs have a strange lower lip, called a mask, which can extend to catch passing prey.

KEY CHARACTERISTICS
ODONATA

- **Proportionally large, compound eyes.**
- **Two pairs of wings with an intricate network of veins.**
- **Antennae short and inconspicuous.**
- **Long, slender body.**
- **Brightly coloured.**
- **Incomplete metamorphosis, with first part of the life cycle spent in water.**

Life cycle

Dragonflies and damselflies undergo incomplete metamorphosis. They lay their eggs in freshwater ponds, lakes and streams. The eggs hatch into nymphs (larvae), which go through a series of moults. After each moult, the nymph becomes more and more like the adult. Finally the mature nymph climbs out of the water and sheds its old exoskeleton, revealing a new one with wings.

Nymph life

The nymphs of dragonflies and damselflies are adapted to living in water. They have gills which allow them to breathe by taking oxygen from the water. The larval stage lasts between one and five years. During this time the nymphs are carnivorous, feeding on a wide range of aquatic animals, from tiny insects to tadpoles. They catch their prey using an extension of the lower lip, called a mask. This has two hooks on the end, a bit like a crab claw. The nymph lies in wait and then shoots out its mask to grab passing prey. It pulls the prey to its jaws, pumps digestive juices into its victim and then sucks up the body fluids.

Adult life

Adult dragonflies and damselflies only live for about a month. Just like the nymphs they are aggressive predators, except unlike the nymphs they hunt in the air instead of the water. Once they have spotted suitable prey, they give chase. To help flight, the dragonfly has sensory hairs on the back of its head, which send information to the brain about the position of the head relative to the thorax. When it gets close to its prey, the dragonfly opens its dangling legs to form a basket and catches the prey.

Hawker dragonflies, such as the emperor dragonfly, patrol stretches of water looking for prey such as small flying insects. These large dragonflies can even tackle butterflies. The darter dragonflies employ a different hunting technique. They perch on a plant stem and watch for prey, darting out to catch it.

Extra order: mayflies (Ephemeroptera)

Mayflies look very similar to damselflies, with their slender body and wings that close over the body. However, the adult and nymph have three distinctive, slender extensions from the tip of the abdomen. The nymphs spend between four months and three years in the water. They are herbivorous, scraping algae from stones and pondweed. Adult mayflies only live for a few days, in which time they have to mate and lay eggs. Many are eaten by fish and birds within hours of emerging from the nymph stage.

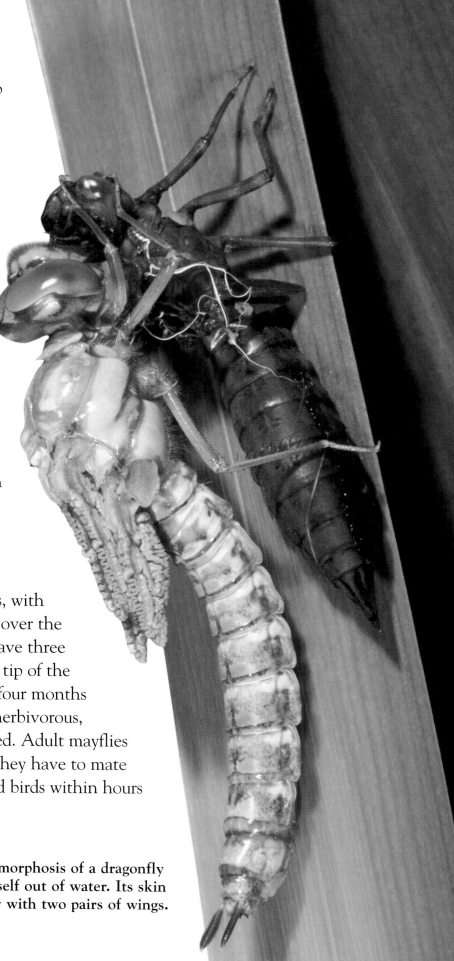

The final stage in the metamorphosis of a dragonfly occurs when the nymph pulls itself out of water. Its skin splits to reveal an adult body with two pairs of wings.

GRASSHOPPERS AND CRICKETS (ORTHOPTERA)

GRASSHOPPERS AND CRICKETS BELONG TO THE ORDER Orthoptera. They are found in most land habitats around the world, except for the very coldest ones. The word Orthoptera means 'straight wings', which refers to the parallel sides of the forewings of these insects.

Orthopterans are best known for their loud chirping sounds, which are heard on sunny summer days and warm evenings. The order Orthoptera consists of more than 20,000 species, including grasshoppers, locusts, crickets, bush crickets (katydids) and mole crickets.

Orthoptera features

The distinctive feature of this order is the extra-long pair of hind legs designed for jumping. These long legs are about three times longer than the other two pairs, and are equipped with powerful muscles. All six legs have claws, which help the insect to grip plants.

Orthopterans have two pairs of wings. The front pair are narrow and leathery, and when the insect is at rest they cover the hindwings. The hindwings are large and very thin, almost see-through. Although these insects can fly, they are more likely to jump, using their wings to help them to travel

The forewings of Orthopterans, such as this blue-winged grasshopper (*Oedipoda caerulescens*), are held out of the way of the hindwings, which have a much larger surface area for flying.

further. Most orthopterans have a pronotum. This is the upper surface of the thorax, which extends forwards over the head.

Singing

The song of these insects is produced by a process called stridulation. This involves rubbing one part of the body (the file) over another part (the scraper). The file has a series of pegs or ridges, which hit the scraper and create the sound. It's a bit like drawing a comb over the edge of a card. The scraper is always on the wing, but the file may be on the leg (as in grasshoppers) or on the opposite wing (as in crickets). Each species has its own distinctive 'song'. The sounds come in bursts or chirps, and are of varying length. The volume and pitch vary, too. Some songs have been likened to the sounds of lawnmowers, sewing machines and even chainsaws! Most of the songs are produced by males in order to attract females. Female grasshoppers also sing, but their song is quieter than that of the males.

Pests

Grasshoppers and locusts have powerful mouthparts with sharp jaws, which are designed to eat tough plant foods. Many are classed as pests because they occur in large numbers and feed on crops, causing a lot of damage. Swarms of locusts regularly appear in parts of Asia, Africa and North America, destroying all crops in their path. Mole crickets are major pests of the lawns and golf courses in the southern USA. They live underground in long burrows. Their forelegs are enlarged and used like a pair of shears, snipping through grass roots.

The female mole cricket (*Gryllotalpa sp.*) lays her eggs in a small, underground chamber. Unlike other species of mole crickets, the *Gryllotalpa* female revisits the chamber to take care of her eggs and hatchlings.

MANTIDS AND COCKROACHES (DICTYOPTERA)

COCKROACHES ARE UNPOPULAR INSECTS BECAUSE MOST people see them in kitchens and hotel rooms, where they are associated with dirt and disease. However, most cockroaches are wild, and do not live or feed near people. Cockroaches are closely related to mantids – insects that catch prey using their long, spiny front legs.

Cockroaches and mantids make up the order Dictyoptera, which means 'net wing'. This refers to the pattern of veins on their forewings. Dictyoptera is divided into two suborders: Mantodea, the mantids, and Blattodea, the cockroaches. Both mantids and cockroaches undergo incomplete metamorphosis.

This female burrowing cockroach (*Blattodea sp.*) is digging a burrow for her egg case. It contains between 12 and 40 eggs, which will develop underground for up to 12 months.

Cockroaches

Cockroaches are ancient insects that first appeared on Earth about 320 million years ago. It is thought that at that time in Earth's history, cockroaches outnumbered all other flying insects. There are far fewer cockroaches in the world today and they are mostly found in the tropics. Of the 4,000 known species of cockroaches, only about 30 are classed as pests.

At first glance, cockroaches look a bit like beetles, with a similar pair of leathery forewings covering the hindwings. However, whereas beetles have forewings that meet exactly in the middle, cockroaches have

forewings that overlap and the female cockroach is often wingless. The body of the cockroach is broad and flattened, and the legs are long and spiny. They have a prominent, shield-like pronotum that extends forwards to cover most of the head. Their sensitive antennae are particularly long and they have large, compound eyes. There are two conspicuous cerci at the end of the abdomen. The females lay eggs, which may be protected within a tough egg case. After a number of weeks, the eggs hatch into nymphs, which look like small, wingless versions of the adults.

Mantids

The 2,000 or so species of mantids live in the tropical parts of the world. They are often called praying mantids because of the way they hold their forelegs as if in prayer. Their head is triangular in shape with powerful jaws. They are the only insects that are able to turn their head to look

Praying mantids are killing machines that have lightning reflexes and spiny,

Scavenging cockroaches

Most cockroaches are nocturnal, but a few are diurnal (active during the day). The majority live on forest floors, but they are also found in caves and homes. A few make their homes in the nests of social insects such as ants. They rely on their antennae to find their way around.

Cockroaches are scavengers, feeding on almost anything that is edible. A few are highly specialized, feeding solely on wood. Wood is indigestible to most animals, so these cockroaches have single-celled organisms living in their gut to help them digest the wood.

Predatory mantids

Mantids are found in a wide variety of habitats, including grassland and woodland. They are usually camouflaged to blend in with their surroundings so they are difficult to spot, for example, the nymphs of the flower mantids are shaped and coloured to look like colourful flowers.

BIGGEST AND SMALLEST

■ The largest known cockroach in the world, the *Megaloblatta longipennis* from Central and South America, has a wingspan of up to 18 cm (7 in).

■ The species *Macropanesthia rhinocerus* from Australia has the largest body, weighing up to 50 g (1.8 oz).

■ The smallest known cockroach is *Attaphila fungicola* from North America, which is only 4 mm (0.2 in) long.

The Oriental cockroach (*Blatta orientalis*) is found in warm places such as kitchens, laundry rooms and hospitals. They emerge at night to scavenge on the remains of food.

Mantids are predators, feeding mostly on other insects, but some of the larger species tackle prey as large as frogs and lizards. They use their camouflage to surprise and catch their prey. Mantids stay very still, waiting for prey to pass close by. When they spot a suitable prey animal, they turn their head to look straight at the animal. Then, in a sudden movement that lasts just a fraction of a second, the mantid reaches out and grabs the prey with its forelegs.

Extra order: Stick and leaf insects (Phasmida)

Stick and leaf insects are often called walking sticks because they resemble sticks, twigs or leaves. There are about 2,500 species, divided between eight families. They are usually green or brown in colour to match the plants in which they hide. Their elongated bodies can reach lengths of 29 cm (11 in) in some species. Stick and leaf insects spend much of their time hanging motionless in plants, shrubs or trees. When they do move they simply sway slightly, as if caught by the movement of the wind. Their powerful jaws are well suited to eating plant leaves. If attacked they can shed their legs, which grow back again when they moult.

This leaf insect has a green body and an outline that blends perfectly with the surrounding leaves. It is almost impossible to spot unless it moves.

TERMITES (ISOPTERA)

TERMITES ARE EASILY CONFUSED WITH ANTS, BUT they are more closely related to cockroaches. Termites are described as social insects because they live together in huge colonies. They are found mostly in the tropical and subtropical parts of the world.

A queen termite is surrounded by workers bringing her food. The queen is so large that she is incapable of moving.

Termites belong to the order Isoptera, which consists of approximately 2,300 species grouped in seven families. Isoptera means 'equal wings', which refers to the similar shape and size of these insects' two pairs of wings.

Living in colonies

Termites live in large groups, called colonies. Each colony can have as many as several million individuals. There is a single queen, a number of kings, and thousands of immature termites who are workers and soldiers. The kings and queen are long-lived, in some cases with a lifespan of up to 50 years, while the workers and soldiers live for only four years. The mature queen has a huge, bloated abdomen up to 10 cm (4 in) long because her role is to lay thousands of eggs each day. The eggs develop into new workers and soldiers.

Unlike bees and wasps, termite workers and soldiers can be either male or female. The workers' job is to collect food for the queen, kings and soldiers, and tend to the nest. Since they are blind, the workers find their way back to the nest by following a scent trail laid down on the outward journey. The soldiers have massive heads packed with muscles that work their curved black jaws. Their role is to protect the colony. The proportion of workers to soldiers depends on the needs of the colony. If the colony is constantly being attacked, more soldiers will be produced but if the nest needs attention, there will be more workers.

Some termites feed on wood and plants but most feed on fungi, which they grow in underground gardens. They bring plant material such as sections of leaf into the nest and the fungi grow on this – just like a large compost heap. Then the termites feed on the fungi.

Massive nests

Termites are the master builders of the animal world. The workers build a nest that extends above and below ground by sticking mud together with saliva. The mound of some nests can rise 7 m (23 ft) or more above the ground level. The chambers containing the eggs and larvae are located deep underground, close to the food stores and fungal gardens. Running up through the middle is a chimney, which is part of the ventilation system.

The termite mound is ventilated as hot air from the underground chambers rises through the central chimney and cooler air is drawn in to replace it.

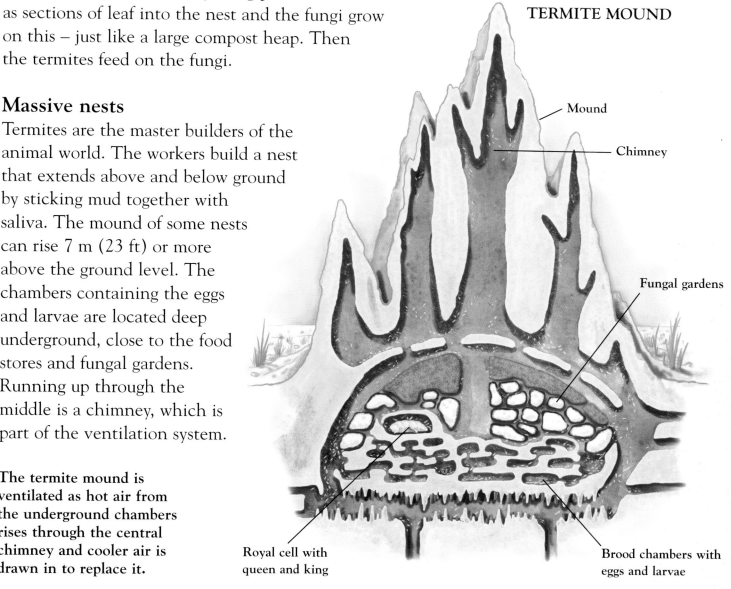

TERMITE MOUND

Mound

Chimney

Fungal gardens

Royal cell with queen and king

Brood chambers with eggs and larvae

EARWIGS (DERMAPTERA)

THE EARWIG WAS NAMED AFTER THE SUPERSTITION THAT it crawls into people's ears as they sleep and bores into their brains. Of course this is completely untrue. However, many earwigs are considered to be pests because they feed on vegetables, fruits and flowers.

The order Dermaptera consists of about 1,900 species of earwigs, which are found around the world. Earwigs range in size from 5–20 mm (0.2–0.8 in) in length and they are coloured brown to black. The word Dermaptera means 'skin-winged', which refers to their soft hindwings. But the earwigs' most distinctive feature is their forceps, or pincers, which are modified cerci at the end of their abdomen. Their forceps make humans think that earwigs are dangerous, but they are harmless to people. The forceps are used to catch prey and to mate. Females have straight forceps, while those of males are curved and more elaborate.

Earwigs have an elongated body and many species are wingless. The winged species have a pair of small forewings that meet in the middle, covering and protecting the hindwings. The hindwings are much larger, fan-shaped and thin. They have to be folded many times to fit under the small forewings. Some winged earwigs are strong fliers, but not all fly regularly.

The earwig (*Forficula auricularia*) raises its forceps over its body like a scorpion when threatened.

Life cycle

Earwigs undergo incomplete metamorphosis, with three stages of growth. The earwig is unusual in the insect world because the female takes good care of her eggs and nymphs. The female lays up to 80 eggs in the soil, which she cleans and guards. The eggs hatch into tiny nymphs, which grow and moult, becoming more like the adult. The female cares for her nymphs until they are able to look after themselves.

Nocturnal activity

Earwigs are nocturnal. During the day they shelter in moist, shady places, under wood piles, stones, boards, and compost piles or in flower beds. They may also be found in potted plants and flowerheads. They come out at night to feed on plants and to scavenge on dead and decaying matter. This is when they can be a nuisance in gardens because they damage vegetables and large flowers.

Large numbers of earwigs can suddenly migrate, gathering together and moving to a new area. There have been reports of hundreds of earwigs moving into crops or even into people's homes.

Some of these earwig eggs have just hatched. The nymphs are small and their exoskeletons are still pale and soft.

KEY CHARACTERISTICS
DERMAPTERA

- Modified cerci that look like a pair of forceps or pincers.
- Winged earwigs have a small pair of forewings and a large pair of hindwings.
- Incomplete metamorphosis.
- Female earwigs care for their eggs and nymphs.

BUGS (HEMIPTERA AND HOMOPTERA)

MANY PEOPLE THINK THAT THE WORD 'BUG' REFERS TO ALL insects. However, the term should only be used when referring to a particular type of insect.

True bugs are sucking insects found all around the world, on land and in water. They range in size from a few millimetres to more than 10 cm (4 in) long. Bugs undergo incomplete metamorphosis. The nymphs look much the same as the adults, except they are much smaller and wingless.

Bugs are classified in two, closely related orders: Hemiptera and Homoptera. Hemiptera contains about 35,000 species, including bedbugs, shield bugs and pond skaters. Homoptera is slightly larger, with about 45,000 species, including cicadas, leafhoppers, aphids and scale insects.

Bugs have piercing and sucking mouthparts. Some suck plant juices and are plant pests, while others are carnivorous and can give humans and other mammals a painful bite. The two orders Hemiptera and Homoptera are considered to include the most destructive species of insects because many are serious pests.

Treehoppers belong to the order Homoptera. They are often called thorn bugs because of their distinctive pronotum, which is shaped like a thorn.

Hemiptera

Hemiptera means 'half wing' and refers to the fact that part of the forewings of these bugs is toughened and hard, while the rest of the forewings and all of the hindwings are membranous (flexible). Both pairs of wings are folded over the flattened body when at rest. Another feature that is characteristic of this order is the mouthparts. These are at the front of the head and consist of four needle-like stylets that rest in a groove called the rostrum. The tip of the rostrum is very sensitive and is used to detect suitable feeding sites. It guides the stylets to the right place and then withdraws as the stylets are inserted into an animal or plant. Food is then sucked up through the stylets.

Homoptera

Homoptera means 'same wing' and refers to the fact that the forewings of these bugs are not divided into two parts. They are either stiff or completely membranous. The wings are held like a roof over the body when the bug is at rest. The mouthparts of these bugs lie below and behind the eyes, so it looks as though they arise from the back of the head or from between the front legs.

The assassin bug (*Reduviidae sp.*) belongs to the order Hemiptera. It is a large, predatory bug that catches, kills and then sucks the body fluids from its victim with its sucking mouthparts.

Habitats

Bugs are found in almost all habitats including ponds, forests and even our own beds! Pond skaters and water measurers have adapted to living and feeding on the surface of water. They have long legs that spread their weight so they do not fall into the water, relying on the water's surface tension to support them. Pond skaters 'row' across the water's surface using their middle legs. Their hind legs trail and act as a type of rudder, leaving their front legs free to catch prey. These insects have hairs that are sensitive to vibrations, which helps them to find struggling insects that have fallen into the water. Water measurers have an elongated head, which is more suited to their method of catching prey – spearing animals living in the water rather than catching animals on the surface of the water.

The adult bed bug (*Cimex lectularius*) is about 5 mm (0.2 in) long when unfed. When fed, the body becomes swollen and elongated.

BED BUGS

Bed bugs share some people's beds. During the day, they hide in crevices in floors, beds or mattresses. They emerge at night to feed on human blood, using their long mouthparts to pierce the skin and suck the blood. Female bed bugs lay about 200 eggs around the bed. The eggs hatch within a few days and the young bugs start feeding straight away.

(Below) This pond skater (*Gerris lacustris*) has caught a bee trapped on the water's surface. The struggles of the bee created ripples in the water, which alerted the pond skater to its presence.

Communication

Cicadas are among the world's noisiest insects. The males are well-known for their song, which can be heard on warm summer evenings in many parts of the world. They sing to attract females and to warn off other males. The song of some cicadas is so loud that it can be heard up to 1.5 km (1 mile) away! Male cicadas have special sound-producing organs on the sides of their abdomen, called tymbals. Each tymbal is attached to an internal muscle, which pulls in and then releases it. As it pops back into position, the tymbal produces a sound.

Pests

Many bugs are pests of plants. One of the most destructive is the aphid, or greenfly. This is a tiny bug with a soft body that feeds on sap from plant stems. Aphids insert their piercing stylets into the plant stem and suck out the sap, which is rich in sugar. Since the plant's growth is reduced, it may die. Aphids have an amazing ability to reproduce, so a few aphids can soon turn into an infestation.

Another pest is the scale insect, or mealy bug, which feeds on plant sap. Heavy infestations of scale insects may seriously weaken a plant. Usually the leaves or fruit are disfigured by the excess wax produced by the female scale insects when they reproduce. The female scale insect is hardly recognizable as an insect because it is often wingless and legless.

Aphids are just a few millimetres long. The wingless adult female aphids can produce 50 to 100 offspring. A newborn aphid becomes a reproducing adult within about a week and can then produce up to five offspring per day for up to 30 days!

BEETLES (COLEOPTERA)

THERE ARE MORE SPECIES OF BEETLES than any other type of insect. There are about 370,000 known species, but more are being discovered all the time, especially in habitats such as tropical rainforests.

To fly, this seven-spotted ladybird (*Coccinella septempunctata*) raises its spotted wing cases to reveal its delicate flying wings underneath.

Beetles are found all around the world and in a wide variety of habitats. There may be as many as 20 different species of beetles living in a city garden and a hundred or more species found living in a few square metres of rainforest. Among the many types of beetle are the well-known ladybird, stag beetle, dung beetle and weevil.

KEY CHARACTERISTICS
COLEOPTERA

- **Toughened wing cases lie over the hindwings.**
- **Powerful biting jaws.**
- **Complete metamorphosis.**

Coleoptera features

Beetles belong to the order Coleoptera. The name Coleoptera means 'sheath wings', which refers to the toughened wing cases that are the beetle's forewings. The wing cases lie over and protect the delicate hindwings, which beetles use for flight. Often the wing cases are brightly coloured, for example the red wings of the cardinal beetle and the sparkly wings of the jewel beetle. Another feature of beetles is the powerful jaws for biting and chewing. Weevils have slightly different heads compared with other beetles. Their head is extended forwards to form a rostrum, which carries the mouthparts.

Moving fast

Although most beetles can fly, they spend little time in the air. Instead they tend to be found on the ground or on plants, hunting for food. Some species of ground beetles do not have hindwings and are restricted to life on the ground. Their legs tend to be longer than other beetles so they can chase insect prey. One group of ground beetles, the tiger beetle, is one of the fastest runners of the insect world. It has been estimated that, relative to their size, some tiger beetles can run faster than cheetahs, travelling at speeds of up to 1 m (3 ft) per second. In contrast, the smaller species of beetles that live in crevices and under bark have short, stubby legs that are more suited to squeezing under bark.

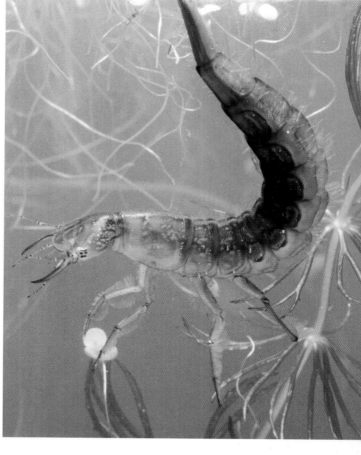

The aquatic larva of the great diving beetle (*Dytiscus marginalis*) has a well-developed head with biting jaws. The larva pushes its tail up above the water to take in oxygen.

Life cycle

Beetles undergo complete metamorphosis with four stages: egg, maggot (larva), pupa and adult. Most larvae are pale, soft bodied, and found in the soil. Some, such as the larvae of ground beetles, are active predators, feeding on small insects. Other beetles, such as the dung beetle, supply their larvae with dung to feed on, whereas the legless weevil larvae hardly move because they are surrounded by their food of plant roots.

Survival

Beetles are a very successful order of insect. Their success comes from their tough exoskeleton and protective wing cases. They can squeeze under stones and leaf litter without injury, survive in dry environments and use their large hindwings to fly.

Desert beetles

Many beetles are found in harsh environments such as deserts, where there is a shortage of water. Their exoskeleton not only protects their body, it reduces the loss of water. Desert-living beetles tend to have long legs to hold their body off the hot sand. Some species have also evolved unique ways of obtaining water, for example the darkling beetle of the Namib Desert, in south-west Africa. In the morning, mists roll over the sandy desert from the ocean, so these beetles climb to the top of sand dunes to obtain droplets of water.

BEETLE FACTS

- One in every three insects is a beetle.
- Stag beetles look quite fearsome, but the heavy antlers of the males are only used for fighting other males.
- The devil's coach horse is a type of rove beetle. It gets its name from the way it raises its abdomen up like a scorpion when threatened.

The male stag beetle (*Lucanus cervus*) has mouthparts that have evolved into enormous jaws. Despite their fearsome appearance, the jaws are useless for biting, and are only used to fight other males.

Aquatic beetles are faced with different problems. An aquatic beetle has to obtain oxygen while it is under water. Adult beetles, such as the great diving beetle, get around the problem by trapping bubbles of air under their wings so they can breathe while they are under water. They have hairs on their hind pair of legs, which help to propel their body through the water. Their aquatic larvae have gills to take oxygen from the water.

Finding food

Most beetles are herbivores, for example leaf beetles and weevils. However, a number are scavengers, including the scarab, stag, rove and carrion beetles. They feed on the dead and decaying bodies of animals and rotting vegetation. Many lay their eggs on rotting vegetation to ensure the larvae have a plentiful supply of food. Carrion beetles lay their eggs on the bodies of dead animals, while dung beetles bury balls of dung with their eggs.

Longhorn beetles are pests of wood. The females use their jaws to chew through bark in order to lay their eggs in the wood. The larvae tunnel through the wood, damaging it as they do so. Some predatory beetles, such as ground beetles, feed on a wide variety of small animals, including other insects. Their jaws are designed to grip and kill prey animals and then chew the body.

(Above) This great diving beetle (*Dytiscus marginalis*) has caught a tadpole. These predatory beetles will also feed on small fish and aquatic insects.

The scarab beetle is a type of dung beetle. It shapes freshly laid dung into a huge ball, which it rolls into an underground nest. The female lays a single egg into each ball. When the eggs hatch, the larvae will feed on the dung.

FLIES (DIPTERA)

FLIES ARE PROBABLY ONE OF THE LEAST-LIKED GROUP OF insects because of the ability of some species to spread disease. They belong to the order Diptera, which contains more than 120,000 different species. Flies are found almost everywhere in the world.

Flies range in size from midges just a few millimetres long to crane flies with a wingspan of 5–6 cm (2–2.4 in). This large order includes fruit flies, houseflies, hoverflies and mosquitoes. It is divided into two suborders according to the length of the antennae. The flies of the suborder Nematocera, such as mosquitoes and crane flies, have long, delicate antennae, while members of the suborder Brachycera, such as blowflies and houseflies, have short, stout antennae.

Hoverflies mimic the appearance of bees and wasps, which have stings, to protect themselves from predators. In fact, hoverflies are harmless. The adults feed on flower pollen and nectar.

Single pair of wings

The word Diptera means 'two wings', which refers to the fact that flies are the only order of insects to have a single pair of wings. The second pair is replaced by a pair of strange, club-shaped organs called halteres. The halteres act as stabilizers, helping the fly's balance in flight, which is essential since flies move very quickly. The characteristic whine of mosquitoes and midges is produced by their rapidly beating wings. Hoverflies, as their name suggests, can hover in front of flowers while they collect nectar, beating their wings very quickly but moving nowhere. Then they dart away at speeds of up to 16 km/h (10 mph). Flies have large compound eyes that occupy much of

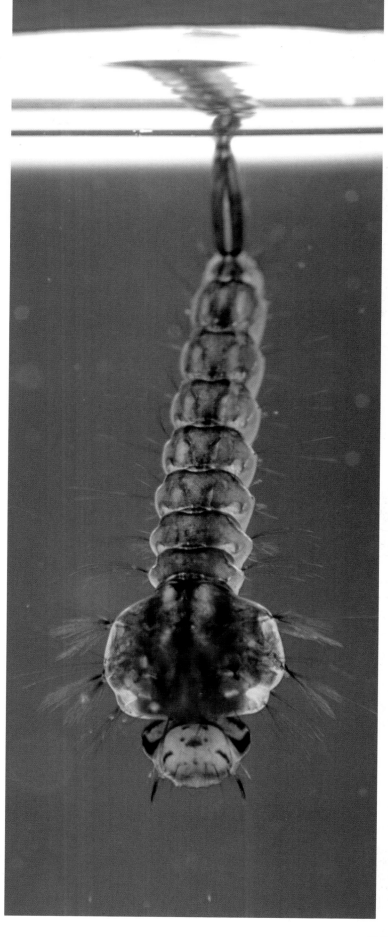

their head. This provides them with excellent vision, which is essential for high-speed flight.

Life cycle

Flies undergo complete metamorphosis with four stages – egg, maggot (larva), pupa and adult. The whole life cycle of a fly can take between one and several weeks, depending on the species and temperature. Their larvae, known as maggots, are legless and almost headless. The maggots turn into pupae, from which the adult flies emerge. Many flies lay their eggs in decaying animal matter and dung. Midges and mosquitoes lay their eggs in water. Some flies are parasites and lay their eggs in the living bodies of other animals. For example, the botfly lays its eggs in the nostrils of mammals such as horses, sheep and goats. The larvae hatch and make their way into the intestines, where they feed and grow. Flesh-flies place their larvae into the wounds of vertebrate animals including humans. They are also parasites of spiders, snails and worms.

The larva of the mosquito lives in water and feeds on organic particles in the water. It uses a breathing tube to get oxygen from the surface.

Food and habitats

One reason that flies are so successful is their ability to adapt and survive in a variety of habitats, and to be able to make use of many different food sources. Flies feed on a range of foods, such as dead animal remains, dung, plant sap and blood. Their mouthparts are adapted for piercing or sucking.

Scorpion flies (*Harpobittacus tillyardi*) are predatory insects. They hang from plants by their front legs, leaving their other legs to catch prey. This one has caught a bee in its hind legs.

Blood suckers

Blood-sucking insects such as mosquitoes have piercing mouthparts that can pass through skin to reach blood vessels. They are dangerous insects because they are carriers of organisms that cause diseases, such as malaria, yellow fever and dengue fever. Only female mosquitoes are blood suckers. In the case of malaria, the female of the *Anopheles*

Blood is sucked out through the mosquito's piercing mouthpart.

The mouthparts of the female mosquito are like needles that pierce the skin and pump saliva into the wound. The saliva contains a substance that prevents blood from clotting, allowing the blood to be sucked out through a central tube.

species of mosquito carries the malarial parasite that is responsible for the disease. This microscopic parasite lives in people's blood. If a female mosquito feeds on the blood of an infected person, she may pick up the parasite and transmit it to the next person she bites.

Liquid feeders

Blowflies and related species have a sucking mouthpart known as a proboscis. When these insects find a food source, they empty the contents of their stomach on to the food to digest it. Once the food has been turned into a liquid, they suck it up. Blowflies feed on many foods, including animal dung and dead animal bodies, picking up bacteria as they feed. They can easily contaminate food in a kitchen.

Predators

A few flies are predators, killing their prey as they suck its blood. Empids or dance flies have a long proboscis, which they use to stab their prey. The proboscis is used to suck the fluids from the animal's body.

Extra order: fleas (Siphonaptera)

Fleas are tiny insects with no wings and a body that is flattened from side to side. Fleas don't have compound eyes. Their most distinctive feature is their very long legs adapted for jumping. Fleas can jump on to passing animals from the ground. Adult fleas are parasites of mammals and birds. They attach to an animal's skin and feed on its blood. After feeding, they drop off. Their larvae feed on dried blood, dead skin cells and other organic debris in nests and dens.

This flea is the human flea (*Pulex irritans*). It prefers human blood but will feed on other mammals too. Infestations of human fleas are less common now that people bathe and wash their clothes more regularly.

33

BUTTERFLIES AND MOTHS (LEPIDOPTERA)

A butterfly emerges from its pupal case. It has to pump blood into its crumpled wings and allow them to dry before it can fly away.

BUTTERFLIES ARE SOME OF THE MOST beautiful insects with their large, colourful wings. They are closely related to moths, and together these two insects form the order Lepidoptera. Butterflies and moths are found in all but the coldest parts of the world. There are more than 165,000 different species, including the monarch, swallowtail and red admiral butterflies, and the atlas and silk moths.

Lepidopteran features

Lepidopterans have two pairs of wings that are linked together. The word Lepidoptera means 'scale wing', after the way the wings of these insects are covered in tiny scales. The scales are arranged in rows, like tiles on a roof. The mouthparts of butterflies and moths form a tube, called a proboscis, which can be coiled up when not in use.

Complete metamorphosis

Lepidopterans undergo complete metamorphosis, with four stages: egg, caterpillar (larva), pupa and adult. Adult butterflies and moths generally only live long enough to mate and for the females to lay their eggs. The eggs hatch into caterpillars, which have a cylindrical body with a head, thorax and abdomen. They have three pairs of legs on their thorax and five pairs of prolegs, or false legs, on their abdomen. The caterpillar is the growing stage and when fully grown, it forms a pupa or chrysalis. This is the stage in which the caterpillar is transformed into an adult butterfly or moth.

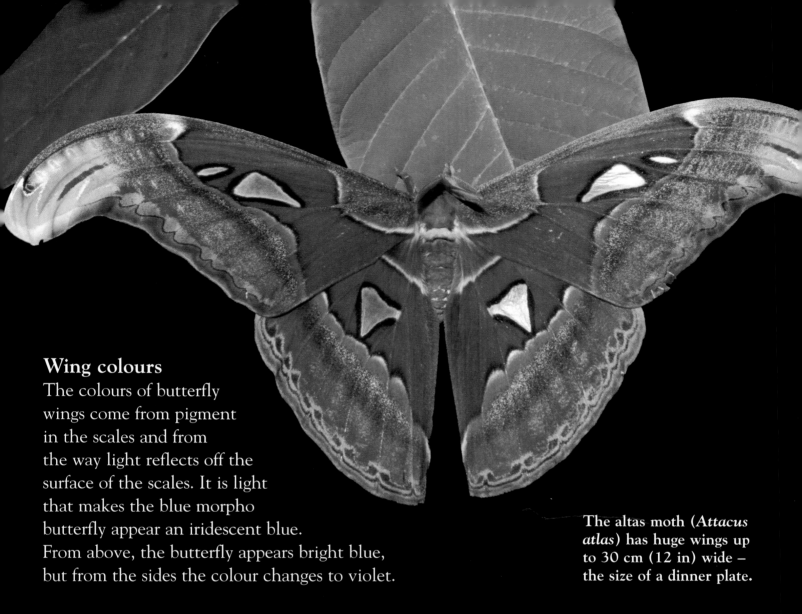

Wing colours

The colours of butterfly
wings come from pigment
in the scales and from
the way light reflects off the
surface of the scales. It is light
that makes the blue morpho
butterfly appear an iridescent blue.
From above, the butterfly appears bright blue,
but from the sides the colour changes to violet.

The altas moth (*Attacus atlas*) has huge wings up to 30 cm (12 in) wide – the size of a dinner plate.

Butterfly or moth?

Butterflies and moths are very similar in appearance and it can
be difficult to tell them apart. In general, butterflies have
clubbed antennae (rounded ends), long, thin bodies and
colourful wings. Usually they settle with their wings upright so
that the undersides are exposed. Moths have fatter, hairier
bodies and their antennae are often feathery,
but never clubbed. When they settle, moths
spread their wings out, with the upper surface
showing. In general, moths' wings are drab in
colour but there are some colourful examples.
Butterflies are diurnal, flying during the day,
whereas most moths are nocturnal, flying at
dusk or through the night.

KEY CHARACTERISTICS
LEPIDOPTERA

■ **Two pairs of wings covered in scales.**

■ **Mouthparts form a proboscis.**

■ **Complete metamorphosis.**

The silver studded blue butterfly (**Plebejus argus**) is found on heathland, where its caterpillars feed on heather and gorse.

Feeding

Adult butterflies and moths feed on nectar produced by flowers. They can reach deep inside the flower with their long proboscis. Caterpillars are very different. They feed on plant leaves, so they are equipped with strong jaws for chewing. Most caterpillars only eat the leaves of a certain plant, or group of plants, known as the food plant. To make sure the caterpillars have enough food, the female lays her eggs only on the leaves of this food plant. Some food plants, such as the nettle, are used by a number of species of butterflies, including the small tortoiseshell, red admiral and peacock. The availability of the food plant can restrict the distribution of some species; for example, the swallowtail is rare in Britain because its food plant, the milkweed, is only found in Norfolk.

The caterpillar of the spurge hawk moth (**Hyles eupheriae**) has strong jaws to chew through tough leaves. It grips each leaf using the legs on its thorax and the prolegs on its abdomen.

Camouflage and warning colours

Butterflies, moths and caterpillars are preyed upon by many animals, especially birds, so they have special ways to avoid their predators. Some rely on camouflage, having colours that blend in with their surroundings. Others rely on poisons and bright colours. The monarch butterfly and the garden tiger moth are poisonous. They have striking black and orange wings to warn predators to stay away. Some caterpillars have false heads and antennae at the end of their abdomen to confuse their predators. The puss moth caterpillar surprises its predators by rearing up and waving its tail.

The caterpillar of the puss moth (*Cerura vinula*) has two tails at the end of its abdomen, which it whips into the air when disturbed by a predator.

Migration

Most butterflies do not fly very far, but monarch butterflies are an exception. They undertake a journey of thousands of kilometres when they fly from their summer breeding grounds to their winter roosting sites. During the summer months, the butterflies breed in the northern states of the USA and in southern Canada. In the autumn, as the weather gets colder, they migrate south to the southern states and Mexico, where they spend the winter roosting in trees. In the spring, the butterflies fly north again to find milkweed, the food plant of their caterpillars.

ANTS, BEES AND WASPS (HYMENOPTERA)

LIKE TERMITES, ANTS, BEES AND WASPS ARE SOCIAL INSECTS that live together in large groups, called colonies. Each colony feeds and cares for its larvae. Ants, bees and wasps are considered to be the most advanced of all the insects. They are found in a variety of habitats such as grasslands, woodlands and gardens.

Membrane wings

Ants, bees and wasps belong to the order Hymenoptera, which consists of about 200,000 species. Other members of the order include ants, honey bees, wasps and ichneumon wasps. The name Hymenoptera means 'membrane-like wings', which refers to these insects' very thin, membranous wings. When they fly, the wings are joined together by tiny hooks. Hymenopterans have both biting and sucking mouthparts. Bees, for example, have a pair of jaws for chewing and a long proboscis for sipping nectar from flowers. All members of this order undergo complete metamorphosis.

Wasps feed their larvae on insects and other invertebrates, so they have powerful jaws and a short proboscis.

Hymenoptera is divided into two suborders: Symphyta and Apocrita. Symphyta is made up of the plant-eating sawflies. Apocrita contains ants, bees and wasps, all of which have a narrow waist between the thorax and abdomen. Female ants, bees and wasps have an ovipositor. This is an egg-laying structure which may also sting.

Workers, drones and queens

Hymenopterans have a complex social structure made up of three classes, or castes. These are queens (fertile females), drones (males) and workers (infertile females). There may be thousands, sometimes millions of individuals in a colony. For example, a typical colony of honeybees consists of a single queen, about 300 male drone bees and about 50,000 worker bees. The queen is the only fertile female and she is much larger than the other females. After mating, she starts laying up to 2,000 eggs a day. Each worker bee has a particular job to do in the colony. Some clean and repair the cells of the hive, while others look after the larvae. Some are responsible for finding food. They leave the nest to find nectar and pollen. Others guard the nest.

Pollination

Ants, bees and wasps have an important role to play in their habitat. Bees, for example, are important pollinators of flowers because they pick up pollen on their hairy bodies as they feed on nectar. The pollen is transferred to the next flower they visit. Without these insects, many flowers would not be able to produce seeds.

The bee-hive is made up of a number of vertical honeycombs divided into thousands of hexagonal cells. The cells are used to store food and rear the larvae.

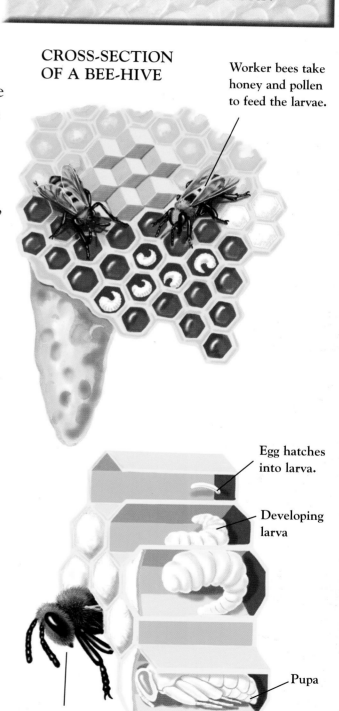

CROSS-SECTION OF A BEE-HIVE

Worker bees take honey and pollen to feed the larvae.

Egg hatches into larva.

Developing larva

Pupa

New adult bee emerges.

Armies of ants

Ants have poor eyesight, so they rely on scent trails to find their
way around. In the rainforest, huge colonies of army ants march
across the forest floor looking for food. There may be as many as
700,000 individuals in a colony of army ants. Each day, raiding
parties of approximately 150,000 ants leave the nest in a long
column up to 100 m (328 ft) long and 8 m (26 ft) wide. The worker
ants are virtually blind, so they follow the trail laid down by the
scout workers. The ants prey on any animal they find in their path,
small or large, insect or mammal. The prey is carried back along the
trail to the nest. Army ants build huge nests in the forest, some of
which extend as much as 6 m (20 ft) below the ground. They stay in
these nests for a few weeks before moving on to a new nesting site.

Communication

As social insects, ants, bees and wasps need to be able to
communicate with each other. Ants communicate using a chemical,
called a pheromone, which they produce from special glands. The
pheromones are used as a form of communication between worker
ants and to mark their trails to the nest.

Meat ants (*Indomyrmex
purpureus*) swarm over
the carcass of a cricket
many times their size.
They tear it to pieces
and carry it back to
their nest.

Worker bees returning to the hive are able to communicate the distance, direction and quality of the food they have found by 'dancing', or flying in a certain pattern. For example, a worker returning from a food source within 25 m (82 ft) of the hive performs a round dance with regular changes in direction. The more changes of direction, the better the quality of the food. If the food source is further away, the worker bee does a waggle dance. In this, the bee moves in a figure of eight. In the middle of the figure, the bee waggles its abdomen from side to side to indicate the distance of the food source. The number of times the bee repeats the dance indicates the quality.

THE FIG WASP AND TREE

The fig wasp and the fig tree could not survive without each other. The female wasp crawls inside the figs and lays her eggs, pollinating the tiny flowers in the process. The figs provide a safe hiding place for the wasp's eggs and the tree benefits, too. Once the flowers have been pollinated, they can produce seeds. The relationship between the fig wasp and the fig tree is an example of mutualism, in which both partners benefit from an association.

Larval food

Bees feed their larvae on pollen and honey. Wasps are predatory animals that feed their larvae on meat. The female potter wasp ensures her larvae get plenty of food by laying her eggs within a clay, pot-shaped nest. She then catches a caterpillar or other prey and puts it in the pot beside the eggs. When the eggs hatch, the larvae feed on the caterpillar. The female ichneumon wasp goes to even greater lengths to provide for her larvae. This wasp lays her eggs in the bodies of other insects. When the eggs hatch, the larvae feed on the bodies of the insects, eventually killing them.

The potter wasp is a solitary wasp. The female builds a tiny nest out of mud to keep her eggs safe.

UNDER THREAT

THERE ARE MILLIONS OF DIFFERENT SPECIES OF INSECTS, but many are under the threat of extinction. The most threatened species are often the larger and more colourful insects, such as butterflies and beetles.

Habitat loss

One of the greatest threats to insects is the loss of their habitat, especially tropical rainforests. Rainforests are home to more species of plants and animals than any other habitat. There are millions of species still undiscovered, many of which are insects. It is likely that some insect species may have become extinct before biologists have had a chance to discover them. Sadly, when one species disappears, others that depend on it may also disappear. For example, at least 100 species of beetles, mites and birds depend on the survival of the army ant (*Eciton burchelli*), which is found in Central and South America.

Many thousands of hectares of rainforest are cleared each year for timber, new farmland and land for building houses and roads.

Modern agriculture

Modern agriculture involves the use of chemicals, such as pesticides, to kill insect pests that damage crops. Often these chemicals kill any insect, not just the pest, so useful insects such as bees and ladybirds are killed, too.

Souvenirs

In many parts of the world, large butterflies and other interesting insects are caught in the wild and sold as tourist souvenirs. Collecting insects from the wild is threatening the survival of some of the more attractive insects. For example, the beautiful birdwing butterflies that are found in the rainforests of southeast Asia are now endangered because of collection and rainforest clearance. Large beetles such as the goliath beetle are also endangered for the same reasons. Fortunately, butterfly breeding centres are being set up by local people so they can breed butterflies rather than catch them in the wild.

Conserving insects

Often the only way to conserve a rare species is to breed it in captivity and then release individuals back into their natural habitat. In Britain, the wart-biter bush cricket and the field cricket are being bred at London Zoo and then released into special protected sites. Similarly, the large blue butterfly has been reintroduced to Britain using butterflies bred in Norway.

Butterflies are collected in the wild and sold as souvenirs to tourists.

BLUE BUTTERFLY

The large blue butterfly (*Maculinea arion*), became extinct in Britain in 1979. Its disappearance baffled scientists because there was plenty of suitable habitat available. Scientists did not realize that its survival depended on a single species of red ants. In 2000, the first reintroductions of these butterflies took place on a number of sites where there were red ants. These reintroductions have proved to be successful and the butterfly is breeding again in Britain.

INSECT CLASSIFICATION

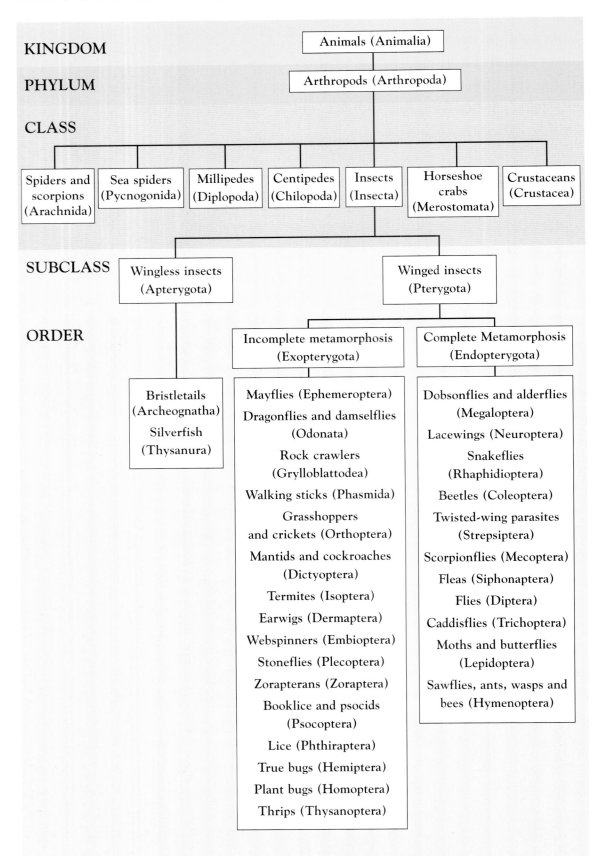

KINGDOM — Animals (Animalia)

PHYLUM — Arthropods (Arthropoda)

CLASS
- Spiders and scorpions (Arachnida)
- Sea spiders (Pycnogonida)
- Millipedes (Diplopoda)
- Centipedes (Chilopoda)
- Insects (Insecta)
- Horseshoe crabs (Merostomata)
- Crustaceans (Crustacea)

SUBCLASS
- Wingless insects (Apterygota)
- Winged insects (Pterygota)

ORDER

Incomplete metamorphosis (Exopterygota)

Complete Metamorphosis (Endopterygota)

Bristletails (Archeognatha)
Silverfish (Thysanura)

Mayflies (Ephemeroptera)
Dragonflies and damselflies (Odonata)
Rock crawlers (Grylloblattodea)
Walking sticks (Phasmida)
Grasshoppers and crickets (Orthoptera)
Mantids and cockroaches (Dictyoptera)
Termites (Isoptera)
Earwigs (Dermaptera)
Webspinners (Embioptera)
Stoneflies (Plecoptera)
Zorapterans (Zoraptera)
Booklice and psocids (Psocoptera)
Lice (Phthiraptera)
True bugs (Hemiptera)
Plant bugs (Homoptera)
Thrips (Thysanoptera)

Dobsonflies and alderflies (Megaloptera)
Lacewings (Neuroptera)
Snakeflies (Rhaphidioptera)
Beetles (Coleoptera)
Twisted-wing parasites (Strepsiptera)
Scorpionflies (Mecoptera)
Fleas (Siphonaptera)
Flies (Diptera)
Caddisflies (Trichoptera)
Moths and butterflies (Lepidoptera)
Sawflies, ants, wasps and bees (Hymenoptera)

GLOSSARY

abdomen The rear part of an insect's body.

adapted Changed in order to cope with the environment.

algae Aquatic, plant-like organisms, including tiny, single-celled organisms and larger seaweeds.

antennae The 'feelers' on an insect's head, used to smell, touch and taste.

aquatic Growing or living in water.

arthropod An invertebrate animal that has an exoskeleton and jointed limbs, such as a crab, spider, insect or centipede.

camouflage Colours and patterns that allow an insect or other animal to blend in with its background.

carnivorous Feeding mainly on the flesh of other animals.

carrion Dead or decaying flesh.

caterpillar The larva of a butterfly or moth.

cerci Structures that extend from the end of the abdomen, seen on insects such as earwigs and bristletails.

colony A large group of insects that live together, for example termites, ants and bees.

compost A mixture of decaying organic matter, such as leaves and food waste.

compound eye An insect eye made up of a large number of tiny units.

contaminate To make impure or unclean.

diurnal Active in the daytime rather than at night.

dung The droppings (faeces) of animals.

evolution A gradual process of change over a long period of time.

exoskeleton The rigid skeleton on the outside of an insect's body.

extinct No longer in existence.

fertile Able to reproduce.

forceps A pair of pincers or tongs, used for grasping.

fungus (plural: fungi) An organism that is neither plant nor animal and is placed in its own kingdom. Yeasts, moulds and mushrooms are all fungi.

gills Organs used to absorb oxygen from water, present in aquatic insect larvae.

habitat The natural environment or home of a plant or animal.

halteres The modified hindwings of flies, which are used as balancing organs.

herbivore An animal that eats mostly plants.

hexagonal Having six sides and six angles.

invertebrate An animal without a backbone, such as an insect, spider or snail.

larva An immature stage in the life cycle of an insect that undergoes complete metamorphosis.

lichen An organism that is made up of an alga and a fungus living together.

lifespan The length of time an animal lives.

maggot Another name for a larva, particularly a fly larva.

mammal A vertebrate animal that is covered in hair and its young are fed milk produced by the female.

GLOSSARY

mask The name given to the extendable lower jaw of dragonfly and damselfly nymphs, which they use to seize prey. It is called a mask because when not in use, it is folded back and covers the mouthparts.

metamorphosis A change in body shape during the life cycle from larva to adult. Complete metamorphosis involves four stages and incomplete metamorphosis has three stages.

migrate To make a regular journey from one place to another.

moult When used in connection with insects, to shed the exoskeleton.

nocturnal Active at night.

nymph The larva of an insect that undergoes incomplete metamorphosis.

omnivore An animal that eats both plant and animal foods.

order A category of organisms in the system of classification, ranking above a family and below a class.

parasite An organism that lives on or in another organism and causes that organism harm.

pheromone A chemical secreted by an insect, to communicate or attract a mate.

phylum The main division of a kingdom in the system of classification, ranking above a class.

pitch The quality of a sound, determined by the number of vibrations producing it.

predator An animal that catches and kills other animals.

prey An animal that is caught and killed by a predator.

primitive At an early stage of evolution or development, for example bristletails are considered to be more primitive than butterflies.

proboscis The long, thin structure used by flies, butterflies and moths to suck up nectar.

prolegs Fleshy structures found on the abdominal segments of insects, which resemble legs.

pronotum The upper surface of the first thoracic segment which may extend forwards over the head in some insects or backwards to cover the whole thorax.

pupa The third stage in the life cycle of an insect undergoing complete metamorphosis.

rainforest Dense forest found in tropical areas near the Equator.

rostrum Mouthparts that look like a beak.

scavenge To feed on dead or decaying matter.

sp. An abbreviation for 'species', used as part of the Latin name for animals where the exact species is unknown.

species A group of living organisms that look similar, which can only breed successfully with each other.

stylets The piercing mouthparts of insects such as aphids.

thorax The middle part of the body of an arthropod, which connects the head and abdomen.

FURTHER INFORMATION

Books

100 Things You Should Know About: Insects and Spiders by Steve Parker (Miles Kelly Publishing, 2004)

Animal: The Definitive Visual Guide to the World's Wildlife editor David Burnie (Dorling Kindersley, 2005)

Animal Classification by Polly Goodman (Wayland, 2007)

Animal Kingdom: Arthropods by Ruth Miller (Raintree, 2005)

Classifying Living Things: Classifying Insects by Andrew Solway (Heinemann Library, 2004)

DK Animal Encyclopedia (Dorling Kindersley, 2006)

The Encyclopedia of Insects and Invertebrates by Maurice Burton & Robert Burton (Little Brown, 2003)

Life Processes series: *Classification* by Holly Wallace (Heinemann Library, 2006)

Living Nature: Insects by Angela Royston (Chrysalis Children's Books, 2005)

The New Encyclopedia of Insects and Their Allies editor Christopher O'Toole (Oxford University Press, 2002)

Nature Files series: *Animal Groupings* by Anita Ganeri (Heinemann Library, 2004)

Science Answers: Classification by Richard & Louise Spilsbury (Heinemann Library, 2005)

Visual Encyclopedia of Animals (Dorling Kindersley, 2004)

Websites

The Animal Diversity Web
http://animaldiversity.ummz.umich.edu
A huge website covering all the animal groups, compiled by the staff and students at the Museum of Zoology, University of Michigan.

BBC Nature
http://www.bbc.co.uk/nature/wildfacts/
Factsheets on hundreds of different species of animals, as well as information about insects in Britain, including metamorphosis and adaptation.

Butterfly Conservation
http://www.butterflyconservation.org/index.shtml
A charity set up to protect native British butterflies from destruction of habitat and other threats.

Creepy Crawlies
http://www.nhm.ac.uk/nature-online/life/insects-spiders
Find out more about all sorts of creepy crawlies at the Natural History Museum, London.

Forensic Entomology
http://www.forensicentomology.com/
Find out how insects can help the police track down criminals.

INDEX

Page numbers in bold refer to a photograph or illustration.

antennae 6, 15, 30, 35
ants 38–39, **40**
aphids 22, **25**
assassin bugs **23**

bed bugs **24**
bees **24**, 38, **39**, 40–41
beetles **26–29**, 42, 43
  carrion 29
  darkling **28**
  diving **29**
  dung 26, 27, **29**
  ground 27, 29
  rove 29
  scarab **29**
  stag 26, **28**, 29
botflies 31, 33
bristletails **6**, 7
burrows **14**
butterflies 5, **34**, 35, **36**, 37

camouflage 16, **17**, 37
caterpillars 34, **36**, 37
cicadas 22, 25
classification 5, 44
claws 12
cockroaches **14**, 15, **16**
collection **43**
colonies 18–19, 38–41
communication 25, 40–41
conservation 43
crickets 12, **13**, **40**, 43

damselflies **5**, 8, **9**, 10–11
disease 30, 32–33
diurnal insects 16, 35
dragonflies 8, 9, **10–11**

earwigs **20–21**
eggs 4, **5**, 10, **19**, 21, 24, 27, 29, 36, 39, 41

empids 33
exoskeleton 4, 6, 10, 28
extinction 42, 43
eyes 4, **8**, **9**, 15, 30

fleas **33**
flies **30–33**
flight 8, 9, 11, **26**, 27, 30, 41
food 7, 10, 16, 20, 29, 32, 33, 36
forceps **20**, 21

gills 10, 29
grasshoppers **12**, 13
greenfly **25**

habitats 7, 16, 24, 26, 28, 32, 38, 39, 42, 43
hoverflies **30**, 33
hunting 11

jaws 27, **28**, **29**, 36, 38

ladybirds **5**, **26**, 43
larvae 4, 10, 19, **27**, 29, **31**, 34, 38, **39**, 41
leafhoppers 22
leaf insects **17**
legs 4, **12**, 13, **15**, 17, 27, **27**, **32**, **33**, 34, **36**
locusts **4**, 13

maggots **27**, **31**
mantids 14, **15**, 16–17
mayflies 11
mealy bugs 25
metamorphosis
  complete 4, **5**, 27, 31, 34, 35, 38
  incomplete 4, **5**, 10, 13, 14, 19, 21, 22,
midges 30, 31, 33
migration 21, 37

mosquitoes 30, **31**, **32**
moths 34, **35–37**
moults 4, 5, 10, 21
mouthparts 13, 22, 23, 24, 25, **28**, **32**, 33, 34
movement 27, 29, 30, 33

nests 18, **19**, **39**, 40
nocturnal insects 7, 21, 35
nymphs 4, **5**, 6, 9, **10**, **11**, 15, **21**, 22

parasites 31, **33**
pesticides 43
pests **13**, 14, **20**, 22, **25**, 43
pollination 39, 41
pond skaters **24**
predators 17, 27, **29**, **32**, 33, 37, 41
prey 8, 10, **11**, 17, 24, **29**, **32**, 41
proboscis 33, 34, 36, 38
pupa 4, **5**, 27, 31, **34**, **39**

reproduction 25

scale insects 22, 25
scavengers **7**, **16**, 21, 29
scorpion flies **32**
silverfish **6**, 7
song 12, 13, 25
stick insects **17**

termites **18–19**
treehoppers **22**

wasps 38, 39, 40, **41**
water measurers 24
weevils 26, 27, 29